Veterans Day

by Mari C. Schuh

Consulting Editor: Gail Saunders-Smith, Ph.D.

Consultant: Tom Dodson
Department of Veterans Affairs
Washington, D.C.

Pebble Books

an imprint of Capstone Press
Mankato, Minnesota

Pebble Books are published by Capstone Press
151 Good Counsel Drive, P.O. Box 669, Mankato, Minnesota 56002
http://www.capstone-press.com

Library of Congress Cataloging-in-Publication Data
Schuh, Mari C., 1975–
    Veterans day / by Mari C. Schuh.
    p. cm.—(National holidays)
    Summary: An introduction to the history, purpose, and observance of Veterans
Day, when we honor men and women who have served in the United States military.
    Includes bibliographical references and index.
    ISBN 0-7368-1655-0 (hardcover)
    1. Veterans Day—Juvenile literature. 2. Holidays—Juvenile literature. [1.Veterans
Day. 2. Holidays.] I. Title. II. Series.
D671.S38 2003
394.264—dc21   2002014484

Note to Parents and Teachers

The National Holidays series supports national social studies standards related to understanding events that celebrate the values and principles of American democracy. This book describes and illustrates Veterans Day. The photographs support early readers in understanding the text. This book also introduces early readers to subject-specific vocabulary words, which are defined in the Words to Know section. Early readers may need assistance to read some words and to use the Table of Contents, Words to Know, Read More, Internet Sites, and Index/Word List sections of the book.

Table of Contents

November

S	M	T	W	T	F	S
						1
2	3	4	5	6	7	8
9	10	11	12	13	14	15
16	17	18	19	20	21	22
23	24	25	26	27	28	29
30						

People in the United States celebrate Veterans Day on November 11.

Veterans Day honors veterans. Veterans are people who served in the United States military.

8

President Dwight Eisenhower
named November 11 as
Veterans Day in 1954.

Some veterans visit schools. They tell students about their work in the military.

People watch parades
on Veterans Day. Some
veterans give speeches.

Many people fly
American flags
on Veterans Day.

Many people visit monuments, statues, and graves on Veterans Day.

THOMAS E GRIX
08 FEB 46 - 15 DEC 67

JAMES P NUGENT
03 APR 51 - 15 DEC 69

ANTHONY J PIERSANTI JR
26 MAY 15 DEC 70

Some people take
a moment of silence
to honor those
who have died.

IN HONOR OF THOSE
WHO SERVED IN THE
KOREAN WAR
1950 — 1953

54,246
108,284
8,177

CHAPTER K.W.

People thank veterans
for being brave.

Words to Know

honor—to show respect or to give praise

military—the armed forces of a country; in the United States, the military includes the Army, Navy, Air Force, Coast Guard and Marine Corps.

monument—a large object that reminds people of an event, a person, or a group of people

serve—to work to help others; people thank veterans for serving in the military because the military protects the country and its people.

statue—a model of a person or an animal made from metal, stone, or wood

veteran—a person who has served in the military; many veterans served in wars.

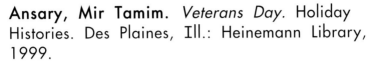

Read More

Ansary, Mir Tamim. *Veterans Day.* Holiday Histories. Des Plaines, Ill.: Heinemann Library, 1999.

Cotton, Jacqueline S. *Veterans Day.* New York: Children's Press, 2002.

Kaplan, Leslie C. *Veterans Day.* The Library of Holidays. New York: PowerKids, 2004.

Internet Sites

Track down many sites about Veterans Day. Visit the FACT HOUND at *http://www.facthound.com*

IT IS EASY! IT IS FUN!

1) Go to *http://www.facthound.com*

2) Type in: 0736816550

3) Click on "FETCH IT" and FACT HOUND will find several links hand-picked by our editors.

Relax and let our pal FACT HOUND do the research for you!

Index/Word List

Word Count: 96
Early-Intervention Level: 14

Credits

Heather Kindseth, series designer; Molly Nei, book designer; Gene Bentdahl, illustrator; Karrey Tweten, photo researcher

AP/Wide World Photos/Ken Cedeno, cover; Cheryl Hatch, 1; Damian Dovarganes, 12; Rich Pedroncelli, 16; Daniel Hulshizer, 18
Capstone Press/Gary Sundermeyer, 10, 14; Nancy White, 20
Corbis/ChromoSohm Inc./Joseph Sohm, 4; Owen Franken, 6
Hulton Archive by Getty Images/Jack Nisberg, 8